Liza Lehmann

In a Persian garden

A song-cycle for four solo voices (soprano, contralto, tenor and bass) with

pianoforte accompaniment

Liza Lehmann

In a Persian garden
A song-cycle for four solo voices (soprano, contralto, tenor and bass) with pianoforte accompaniment

ISBN/EAN: 9783741173479

Manufactured in Europe, USA, Canada, Australia, Japa

Cover: Foto ©Angelika Wolter / pixelio.de

Manufactured and distributed by brebook publishing software (www.brebook.com)

Liza Lehmann

In a Persian garden

TO MY HUSBAND.

IN A PERSIAN GARDEN.

A Song-Cycle

FOR FOUR SOLO VOICES

(SOPRANO, CONTRALTO, TENOR, AND BASS),

With Pianoforte Accompaniment.

THE WORDS SELECTED FROM THE
RUBAIYÁT
OF
OMAR KHAYYÁM
(FITZGERALD'S TRANSLATION)

By kind permission of Messrs. MACMILLAN & CO.

THE MUSIC COMPOSED BY
LIZA LEHMANN.

Copyright, 1896, by
Metzler & Co., Ltd.

Price 5s. net.

London:
METZLER & CO., Ltd., 42, Great Marlborough St., W.

CONTENTS.

		PAGE
QUARTETTE. "Wake! for the sun who scatter'd into flight"	...	2
SOLO TENOR. "Before the phantom of false morning died"	...	4
RECITATIVE (Bass). "Now the new year reviving old desires"	...	8
SOLO TENOR. "Iràm indeed is gone with all his rose"		9
QUARTETTE. "Come, fill the cup, and in the fire of Spring"	...	10
SOLO BASS. "Whether at Naishapur or Babylon"	...	14
CONTRALTO (Recitative). "Ah, not a drop that from our cups we throw"	...	18
CONTRALTO SOLO. "I sometimes think that never blows so red"	...	19
DUET (Soprano and Tenor). "A book of verses underneath the bough"	...	21
BASS SOLO. "Myself when young did eagerly frequent"	...	25
BASS (Recitative). "Ah, make the most of what we yet may spend"	...	30
CONTRALTO SOLO. "When you and I behind the veil are past"	...	30
SOPRANO (Recitative). "But if the soul can fling the dust aside"	...	31
SOPRANO SOLO. "I sent my soul through the invisible"	...	32
TENOR SOLO. "Alas! that Spring should vanish with the rose!"	...	37
CONTRALTO SOLO. "The worldly hope men set their hearts upon"	...	39
SOPRANO SOLO. "Each morn a thousand roses brings, you say"	...	43
QUARTETTE. "They say the lion and the lizard keep"	...	45
TENOR (Recitative). "Ah, fill the cup! what boots it to repeat"	...	60
TENOR SOLO. "Ah, moon of my delight, that knows no wane"	...	63
BASS SOLO. "As then the tulip for her morning sup"	...	70
QUARTETTE. "Alas! that Spring should vanish with the rose"	...	74

IN A PERSIAN GARDEN.

QUARTETTE.
(Soprano, Contralto, Tenor, Bass.)

Wake! For the Sun who scatter'd into flight
The Stars before him from the field of night,
Drives night along with them from Heav'n, and strikes
The Sultan's turret with a shaft of Light.

(SOLO TENOR.)

Before the phantom of false morning¹ died
Methought a voice within the Tavern cried:
"When all the Temple is prepared within
Why nods the drowsy Worshipper outside?"

RECITATIVE (BASS).

Now the new year² reviving old Desires,
The thoughtful Soul to Solitude retires,
Where the "White Hand of Moses"³ on the Bough
Puts out, and Jesus from the Ground suspires.

(SOLO TENOR.)

Irám⁴ indeed is gone with all his Rose,
And Jamshyd's⁵ sev'n-ring'd Cup where no one knows;
But still a Ruby kindles in the Vine,
And many a Garden by the water blows.

QUARTETTE.
(Soprano, Contralto, Tenor, Bass.)

Come, fill the Cup, and in the fire of Spring
Your Winter-garment of Repentance fling.
The Bird of Time has but a little way
To fly—and lo, the Bird is on the wing!

(SOLO BASS.)

Whether at Naishapur or Babylon,
Whether the Cup with sweet or Litter run,
The Wine of Life keeps oozing drop by drop,
The Leaves of Life keep falling one by one.

---

¹ The "false dawn," *subh-i-kázib*, a transient light on the horizon about an hour before the *subh-i-sádik*, or "True dawn": a well-known phenomenon in the East.
² Beginning with the Vernal Equinox.
³ The "White Hand of Moses," Exodus iv. 6; where Moses draws forth his hand, not leprous as in the Persians' Legends as Moses, but white as our Shepherdesses in Spring. Perhaps, according to these, also the healing Power of Jesus touched in his threads.
⁴ Irám, a garden, planted by King Shaddád, and now sunk somewhere in the sands of Arabia.
⁵ Jamshyd's sev'n-ring'd cup was typical of the Seven Heavens, Seven Planets, Seven Seas, &c., and was a Divining Cup.

CONTRALTO (*Recitative*).

Ah, not a drop that from our Cups we throw
For Earth to drink of,[1] but may steal below,
To quench the fire of Anguish in some Eye
There hidden, far beneath, and long ago.

(CONTRALTO SOLO.)

I sometimes think that never blows so red
The Rose as where some buried Cæsar bled;
That ev'ry Hyacinth the Garden wears
Dropt in her lap from some once lovely head.

And this reviving Herb, whose tender green,
Fledges the river—lip on which we lean,—
Ah—lean upon it lightly—for who knows
From what once lovely Lip it springs unseen.

DUET.

(*Soprano and Tenor.*)

A Book of Verses underneath the Bough,
A Jug of Wine, a Loaf of Bread—and Thou
Beside me singing in the Wilderness—
Ah, Wilderness were Paradise enow !

(BASS SOLO.)

Myself when young did eagerly frequent
Doctor and Saint and heard great argument—
 . . . . . . but evermore
Came out by that same door where in I went.

With them the Seed of Wisdom did I sow,
And with my own Hand labour'd it to grow,
And this was all the Harvest that I reap'd,
"I came like Water, and like Wind I go."

Why, all the Saints and Sages who discuss'd
Of the two Worlds so learnedly, are thrust
Like foolish Prophets forth ; their words to scorn
Are scatter'd, and their mouths are stopp'd with Dust.

(BASS RECITATIVE.)

Ah, make the most of what we yet may spend,
Before we too into the Dust descend !

(CONTRALTO SOLO.)

When you and I behind the veil are past
Oh, but the long, long while the World shall last—

---

[1] The custom of throwing a little wine on the ground before drinking still continues in Persia.

(SOPRANO RECITATIVE.)
But if the Soul can fling the Dust aside
And naked on the air of Heaven ride,
Were't not a shame—were't not a shame for him
In this clay carcase crippled to abide?

SONG.

I sent my Soul through the Invisible,
Some secret of that after-life to spell,
And by-and-bye my Soul return'd to me
And answer'd: I myself am Heav'n and Hell.

Heav'n but the vision of fulfilled Desire
And Hell the Shadow from a Soul on fire,
Cast on the Darkness into which ourselves,
So late emerged from, shall so soon expire.

(TENOR SOLO.)
Alas! that Spring should vanish with the Rose!
That youth's sweet-scented manuscript should close!
The Nightingale that in the Branches sang,
Ah, whence and whither flown again who knows?—

(CONTRALTO SOLO.)
The worldly hope men set their Hearts upon
Turns Ashes, or it prospers; and anon
Like Snow upon the Desert's dusty face,
Lighting a little hour or two—is gone.

Think, in this batter'd Caravanserai,
Whose Portals are alternate Night and Day,
How Sultan after Sultan with his Pomp,
Abode his destined hour and went his way.

Waste not your hour!

(SOPRANO SOLO.)
Each morn a thousand Roses brings, you say;
Yes,—but where leaves the Rose of yesterday?—
And this first Summer month that brings the Rose,
Shall take Jamshyd* and Kaikobád† away.

QUARTETTE.
(*Soprano, Contralto, Tenor, Bass.*)
They say the Lion and the Lizard keep
The Courts where Jamshyd gloried and drank deep,
And Bahrám, that wild Hunter,—the wild Ass
Stamps o'er his Head, but cannot break his sleep.

* Jamshyd, the "King Splendid" of the Peshdadian dynasty.
† King Kaikobád, called "the Great."

Lo, some we lov'd, the loveliest and best
That from his Vintage rolling time has prest,
Have drunk their Cup a round or two before,
And one by one crept silently to rest.

Strange, is it not, that of the myriads who
Before us pass'd the Door of Darkness through,
Not one returns to tell us of the Road
Which to discover we must travel too.

(Tenor Recitative.)
Ah, fill the Cup! What boots it to repeat
How time is slipping underneath our Feet.

Better be jocund with the fruitful Grape
Than sadden after none, or bitter Fruit.

Ah, Love, could you and I with Fate conspire
To grasp the sorry Scheme of things entire,
Would we not shatter it to bits—and then
Remould it nearer to the Heart's Desire!

(Tenor Solo.)
Ah, Moon of my Delight, that knows no wane,
The Moon of Heav'n is rising once again—
How oft hereafter rising shall she look
Through this same Garden after me—in vain.

And when thyself with shining Foot shall pass
Among the Guests Star-scatter'd on the Grass,
And in thy joyous Errand reach the Spot
Where I made one—turn down an empty Glass!

(Bass Solo.)
As then the Tulip for her morning sup
Of Heav'nly Vintage from the Soil looks up,
Do you devoutly do the like, till Heav'n
To Earth invert you—like an empty Cup.

So when that Angel of the darker Drink,
At last shall find you by the river-brink,
And, offering his Cup, invite your Soul
Forth to your Lips to quaff—you shall not shrink.

Quartette.
(Soprano, Contralto, Tenor, Bass.)
Alas, that Spring should vanish with the Rose,
That Youth's sweet-scented Manuscript should close!
The Nightingale that in the Branches sang,
Ah, whence and whither flown again, who knows!

Finis.

"IN A PERSIAN GARDEN."

A
SONG-CYCLE.

* The Words selected from The Rubáiyát of
OMAR KHAYYÁM.

The Music by
LIZA LEHMANN.

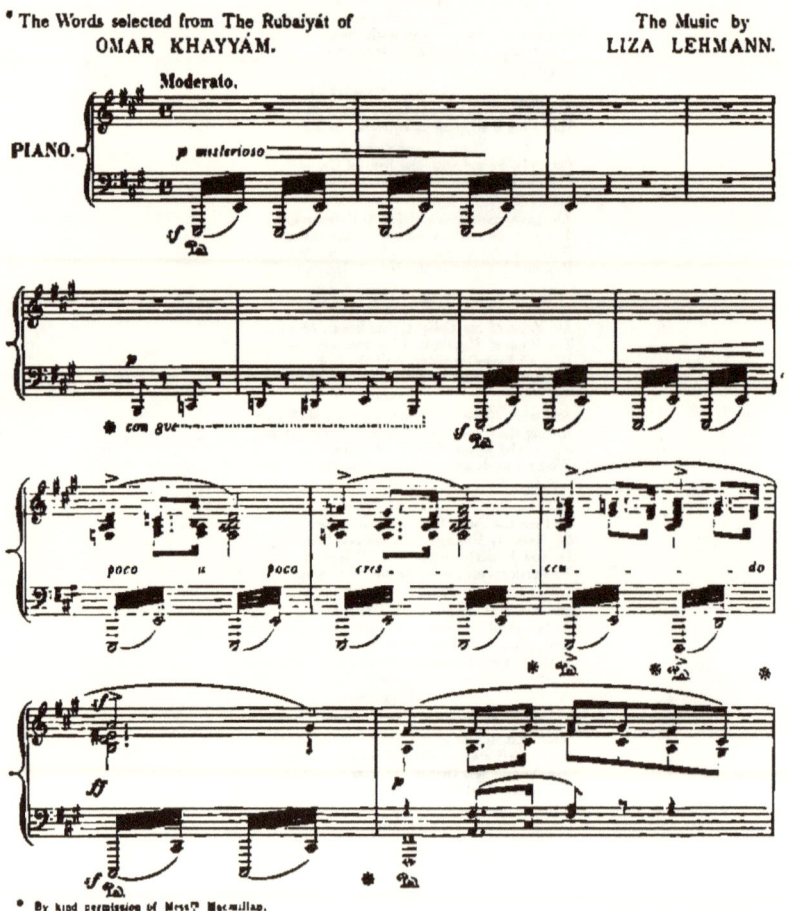

* By kind permission of Messrs. Macmillan.

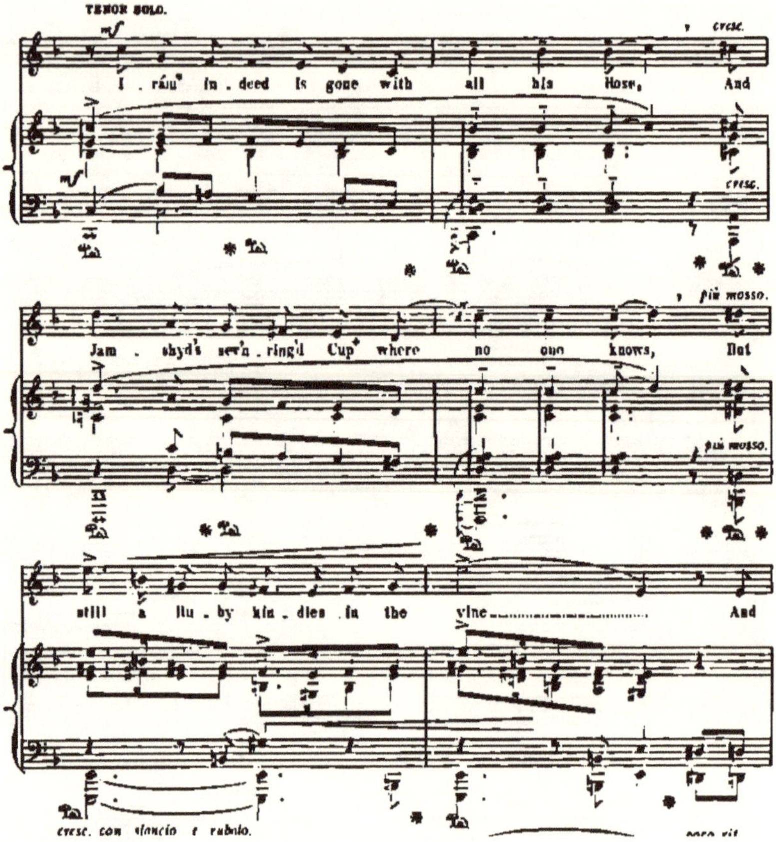

TENOR SOLO.

I- ráml in- deed is gone with all his Rose, And Jam- shyd's sev'n ring'd Cup where no one knows, But still a Ru- by kin- dies in the vine.............. And

cresc. con slancio e rubato.   *poco rit.*

14

CONTRALTO SOLO.

Espressivo, ma non troppo lento.

Ah! not a drop that from our Cups we throw For earth to drink of* but may steal be-

-low...... To quench the fire...... of an-guish in some eye There

bid-den far be-neath...... and long a-go.

cantabile
pp

Andante.
dolce.
dolce.

* The custom of throwing a little wine on the ground before drinking still continues in Persia.

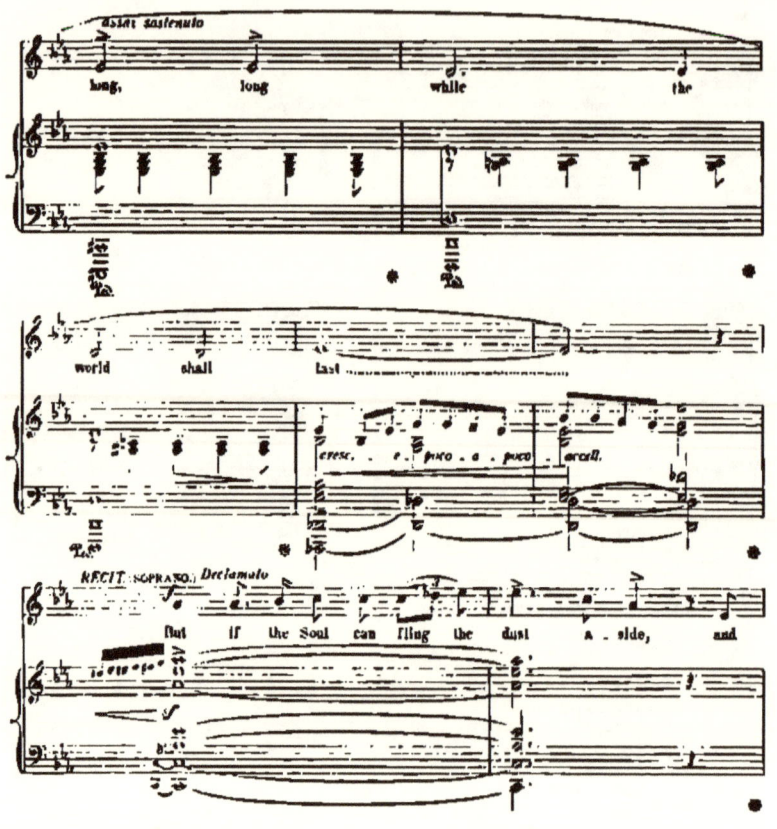

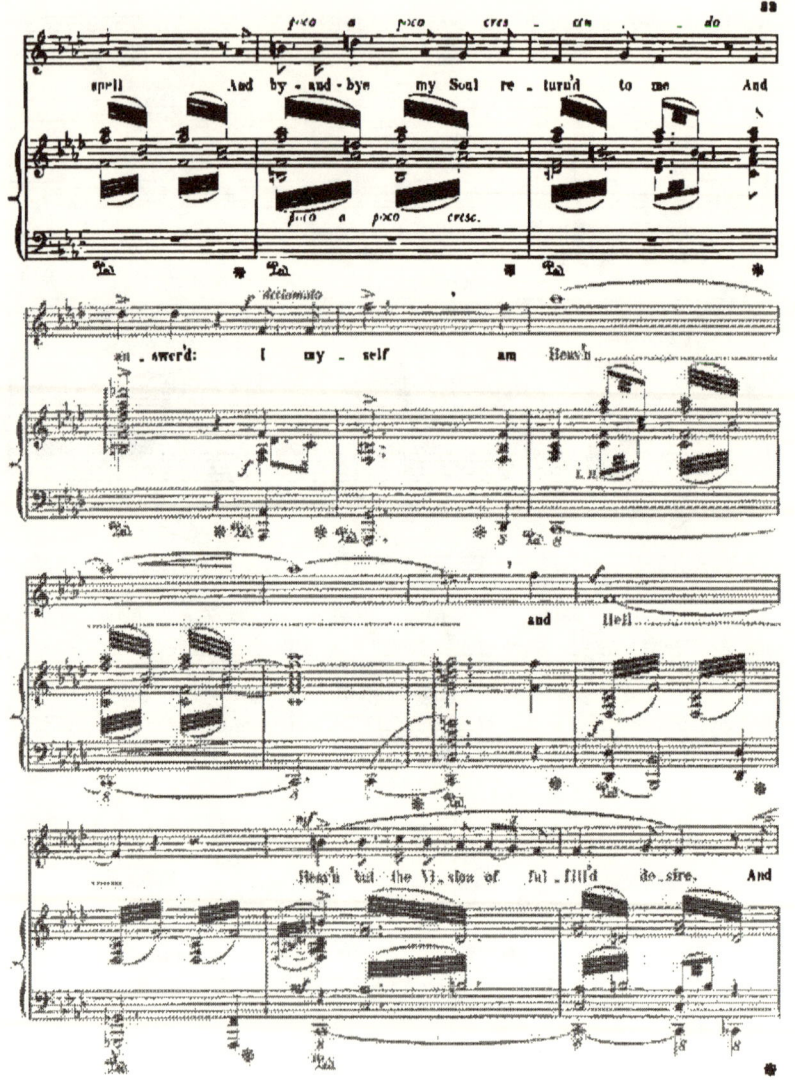

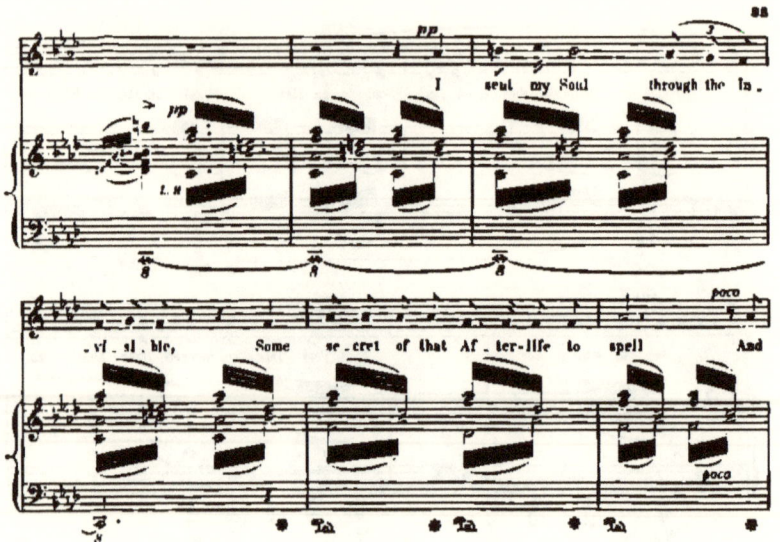

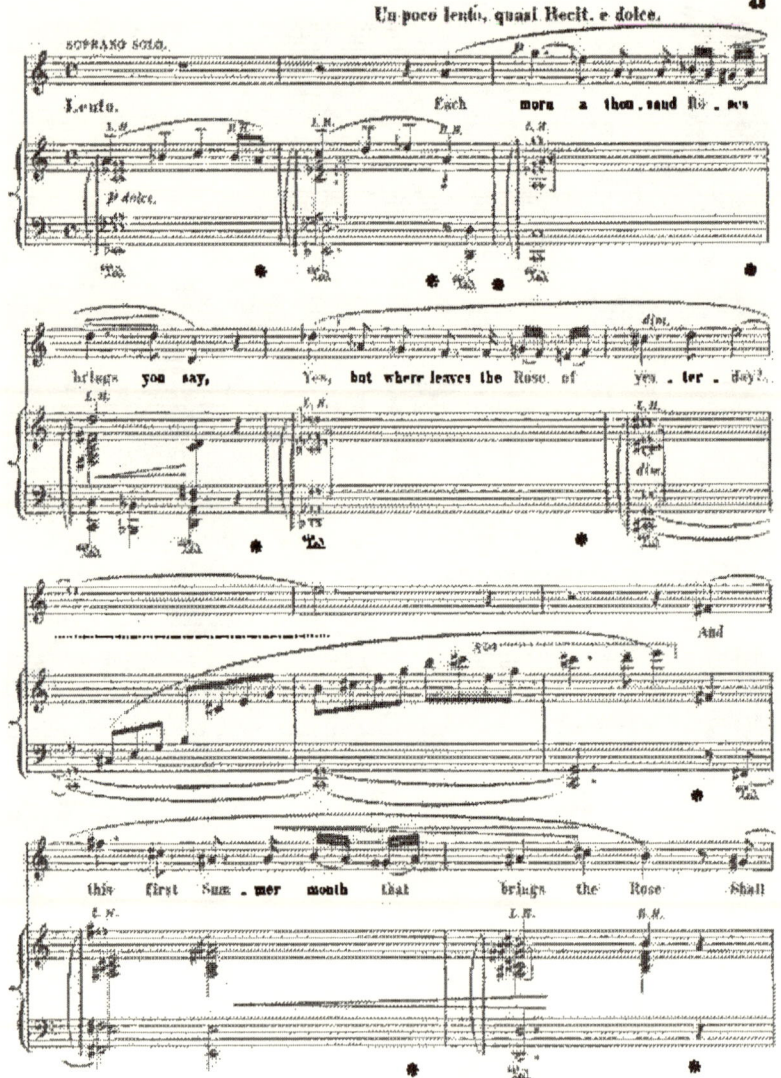

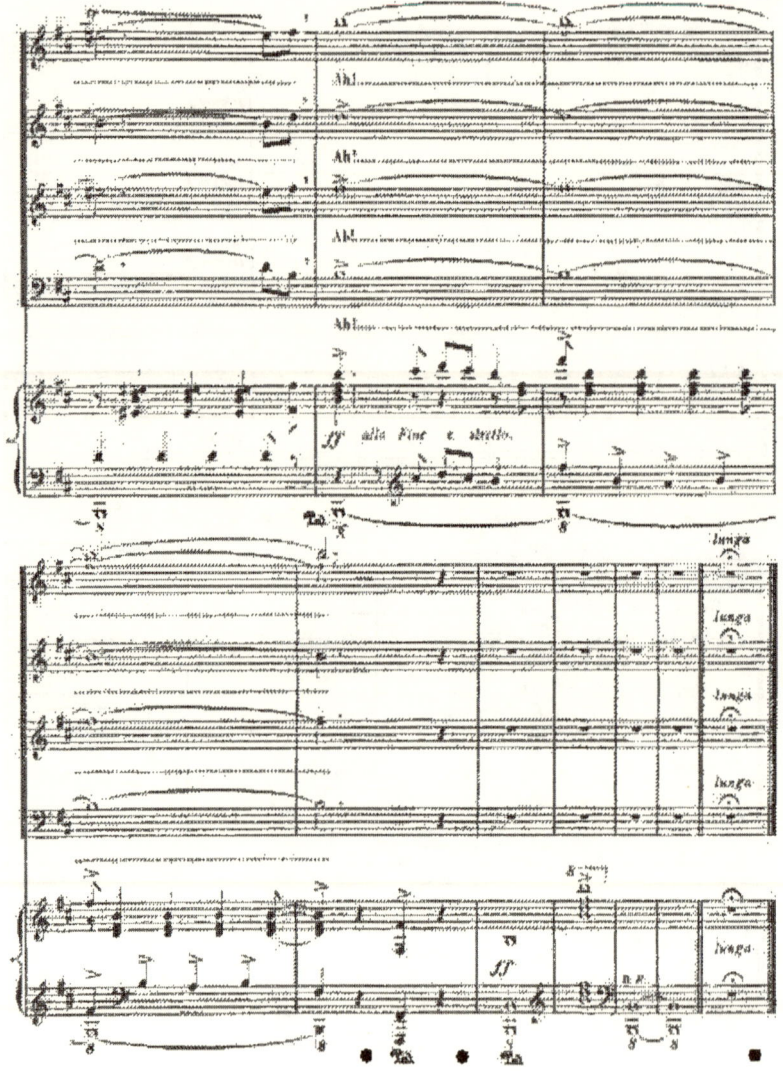

METZLER'S ALBUMS
OF
ARTISTIC SONGS.

A. GORING THOMAS.
ALBUM OF THIRTEEN SONGS.
Price 5/- net.

CONTENTS:

No.		
1.	Jours et Vieux (Old Age and Youth)	H. Carrington Watson
2.	Le Bonheur (Regnesus)	
3.	Chanson d'Avril (Bouel)	Remy Belleau, Wakam Rambugs
4.	Sa j'etais Roi (Were I a king)	Victor Hugo
5.	Consolation (Ransonsaul)	Thos. Marzials, Victor Hugo
6.	Mon Petit Croat (My Little Corset)	Jules Truvaileul, Beranger
7.	La Captive (The Captive)	Victor Hugo
8.	Chanson a Boire (Drinking Song)	Thos. Marzials, Musset
9.	La Sultane Favorite (The Favourite)	Victor Hugo
10.	Les Papillons (Butterflies)	Thos. Marzials, Theophile Gautier
11.	Serenade (A Serenade)	Thos. Manado
12.	Chanson de Barberine (Rapouse - Song)	Thos. Marzials, Alfred de Musset, William Mariage
13.	Sober Kaloprond (Youri)	from Kerner's "Laker" Thos. Marzials

F. H. COWEN.
ALBUM OF NINE SONGS. Words by LONGFELLOW.
Price 2/6 net.

CONTENTS:

No.		No.	
1.	Stay at home	6.	The sea hath its pearls
2.	Love, what wilt thou with this heart of mine?	7.	My lady sleeps (Serenade)
3.	The light of stars	8.	Sundown
4.	It is not always May	9.	Onaway! awake, beloved (from "Hiawatha")
5.	Eyes so trustful		

F. H. COWEN.
ALBUM OF SACRED SONGS.
Price 4/- net.

CONTENTS:

No.		No.	
1.	The Kerry Shore	4.	Evening Hymn
	Words by Author of "John Halifax"		Words by Adelaide Procter
2.	Light in Darkness (With Organ Obbligato ad lib.)	5.	Passing away (With Organ Obbligato ad lib.)
	Words from The Queen		Words by Mrs. Hemans
3.	The Pilgrim		
	Words by Adelaide Procter		

ALFRED CELLIER.
ALBUM OF SIX SONGS, written by M. C. STEPHENSON.
Price 3/- net.

CONTENTS:

No.		No.	
1.	All men deceivers	4.	The Game of Love
2.	Mine! all mine	5.	Time up, my Late
3.	Song of the Night	6.	Song of the Lute

LIZA LEHMANN.
A SONG-CYCLE, ENTITLED
"IN A PERSIAN GARDEN."
Price 5/- net.

CONTENTS:

QUARTETTE—Wake! for the sun who scatter'd into flight.
SOLO, TENOR—Before the phantom of false morning died.
RECIT. (Bass)—Now the new year reviving old desires.
SOLO, TENOR—Iram indeed is gone with all his rose.
QUARTETTE—Come fill the cup, and in the fire of spring.
SOLO, BASS—Whether at Naishapur or Babylon.
CONTRALTO SOLO (in recit.), and A long kiss from rosy lips we throng.
CONTRALTO SOLO—I sometimes think that never blows so red.
RECIT. (Tenor) and SOLO—Ah, leaf of a rose under-neath the bough.
BASS SOLO—Myself, when young, did eagerly frequent.
SOLO (Bass)—Ah, make the most of what we yet may spend.
CONTRALTO SOLO—Whay you that I find that neither are just.
SOPRANO (Recit.)—But if the soul can fling the dust aside.
SOPRANO SOLO—I sent my soul through the invisible.
TENOR SOLO—Alas! that spring should vanish with the rose.
CONTRALTO SOLO—The wealth to the mortal their hearts open.
SOPRANO SOLO—Each morn a thousand roses brings, you say.
QUARTETTE—They say the lion and the lizard keep.
TENOR (Recit.)—Ah, fill the cup; what boots it to repeat.
TENOR SOLO—Ah, moon of my delight, that knows no wane.
BASS SOLO—As then the tulips for morning sup.
QUARTETTE—Ah! this spring should vanish with the rose.

ADELA MADDISON.
ALBUM OF TWELVE SONGS.
Price 2/6 net.

CONTENTS:

Opus 9	No.		Opus 9	No.	
	1.	Bleak Weather		7.	A little while
	2.	Before Sunset		8.	Cinq annees
	3.	The Triumph of Time		9.	Oh, that 'twere possible
	4.	A Stage Love	Opus 10.	No.	Larte
	5.	An Interlude		1.	
	6.	Repose		2.	Au clair moon

LAWRENCE KELLIE.
ALBUM OF TEN SONGS.
Price 4/- net.

CONTENTS:

No.		No.	
1.	As love is new	7.	Then Queen
2.	Ask me no more	8.	Fettered by Fate
3.	Far away in a land	9.	The lowland maggie with the tree
4.	To heart! to horse!	10.	A Dirge
5.	The day has a thousand joys		
6.	Ya ask me why I lac		

LAWRENCE KELLIE.
ALBUM OF EIGHT SONGS.
Price 3/- net.

CONTENTS:

No.		No.	
1.	All through a summer land	5.	Urban Serenade
2.	Love's Birthday	6.	Apple Blossom
3.	Is this life	7.	Now, what is love
4.	The Fairyland	8.	Eastride

METZLER & CO., Ltd., 40 to 43, Great Marlborough Street, London, W.

www.ingramcontent.com/pod-product-compliance
Lightning Source LLC
Chambersburg PA
CBHW020308090426
42735CB00009B/1273